BECOME AN INCREDIBLE NEW YOU

POWER DRESSING SECRETS FOR ENTREPRENEURS, PROFESSIONALS AND INDIVIDUALS

BECOME AN INCREDIBLE NEW YOU

POWER DRESSING SECRETS FOR ENTREPRENEURS, PROFESSIONALS AND INDIVIDUALS

BANNYA BASU

Worldwide Published by
Pendown Press

PENDOWN PRESS

An ISO 9001 & ISO 14001 Certif ed Co.,
Regd. Off ce: 2525/193, 1st Floor, Onkar Nagar-A,
Tri Nagar, Delhi-110035
Ph.: 09350849407, 09312235086
E-mail: info@pendownpress.com
Branch Off ce: 1A/2A, 20, Hari Sadan, Ansari Road,
Daryaganj, New Delhi-110002
Ph.: 011-45794768
Website: PendownPress.com

First Edition: 2021

ISBN: 978-93-90557-44-8

Contents

MY JOURNEY

I am Bannya Basu, a certified image consultant, soft-skill facilitator and corporate trainer. I am running a successful image consulting and soft-skill training company for the last five years; this has given me a larger purpose to serve people across the globe.

In addition to the professional qualifications, my background in the hospitality industry perfectly blends with the business of image management. I have combined experience of 14 years with Taj Bengal and Air India, in the latter as a cabin crew. Both these assignments helped me gain knowledge of how well-dressed, well-groomed, well-mannered personality and sharp communication skills make the difference.

You have to present yourself as the best in this highly-competitive era. I believe, when you feel confident and look good, then you are more likely to succeed both on professional and personal fronts.

My company, "Bannya Basu Image Consulting" is born out of a strong desire to make a difference in people's lives. Over the years, I have successfully used various image makeover tools and techniques to help more than 700 people feel confident about themselves—the way they look, feel and act.

The journey so far has been satisfying.

–Bannya Basu

IMAGE MAKEOVER

HOW IT CAN HELP YOU?

Do any of the following situations sound familiar to you?

- You feel uncomfortable at corporate meetings or social events and struggle to strike up a conversation.

- Your image is not matching your business status or a new job.

- You often feel that others get more opportunities even though you might be more deserving.

- You constantly feel that your look, style and communication are inferior, and you are not getting noticed by people.

- You are tired and bored of clothes you have in your wardrobe and want to update and build a mix-and-match wardrobe with variety without investing a lot of money, time and effort.

- Your appearance anxiety holds you back from meeting people and gaining their trust.

Earlier only celebrities, elite class and politicians used to hire Image Consultants to look good and dress in style, but in today's world, it is not a choice, it's rather a necessity. It's a cut-throat competition out there. Each one of us needs to present an image that is powerful and gets you ahead in life.

If you don't present yourself in the best way you could, chances are you will miss out on opportunities you crave for.

You may not worry about your appearance and its impact but people around you form an impression in their minds about your personality, ability and credibility.

Would you be happy to let your appearance—online and in-person and hold you back from getting the success you deserve or would you like to transform it inside out?

" Your shadow can leave you at times but your image does not and that is where Image Management helps you become your true self."

WHY YOU SHOULD READ THIS MINI-BOOK?

Now you must be wondering why this free book when I could have charged a premium for sharing my knowledge and expertise with you?

In my 19 years of work experience, I have seen people who are confident in their look, feel and act are more likely to succeed both in their professional and personal lives.

Remember, the most common thing in this world is unsuccessful brilliant people because they fail to create an image of confidence.

I am on a mission to help millions of people who truly deserve to live an extraordinary life. It's not possible for me to coach everyone personally due to time constraints, so, this is a gift to all the people who want to stand out in the crowd, get a better position, and feel more respected, noticed or heard.

I hope this mini-book will help you fulfill your goal and achieve success in all walks of life.

IMAGE MAKEOVER

One of the most important facets which affect your credibility and success level is "How you present yourself"; your presentation style speaks a lot about your personality.

You might be having certain skills, abilities and experiences, but people often judge just by looking at your appearance, and based on that they also decide whether to build a relationship with you or just move on. You might have different roles, goals and vocations but I'm sure you want to climb success ladders in your respective field.

Success comes when two things happen simultaneously.

First, you must get an opportunity.

Second, the day you get that opportunity, you must perform well.

Unless both these happen simultaneously, you cannot really achieve much in life. While your performance depends on your skills, experiences and abilities, getting that opportunity largely depends on creating a great positive first impression.

We know that the first impression is formed within seven seconds of meeting any person. In those seven seconds, you communicate a lot about your personality, friendliness, confidence and financial status. First impressions are not reversible and undone easily. Therefore, it is imperative to take care of creating the first impression.

Now, the key question is: on what basis are these first impressions formed?

People form the first impression on the basis of your appearance, clothing, grooming, body language, etiquette and communication.

Creating a good first impression is not onetime process, it's an ongoing process.

Although, you must present yourself in the best way you could, it becomes extremely important in every threshold situation—it is a point of transition when you start something new or shift from one role to another in life. Starting a business, moving to a professional role after a sabbatical, getting promoted or getting married, all these are the common threshold situations in life.

People face different threshold situations according to their lifestyle, and that's the time it becomes important for them to improve their image in terms of appearance, behaviour and communication; this is also known as "appearance management."

"Appearance management" is also called image management or image makeover.

Chapter 1

POWER UP YOUR CURRENT WARDROBE

Many times, you ignore the fact that clothes don't matter. But, they really matter!

This attitude is proper in times of survival or extreme emergency when you don't care about your appearance. In your daily life, clothes make a positive contribution. Knowing that clothing is one of the basic necessities, why not choose the clothes in such a way that apart from meeting your needs, they could help you achieve your goals too.

You and I are born without any pre-conceived notion about ourselves. As we grow old, we develop a body image based on the compliments and criticisms that we receive from others from time-to-time. Body image plays an important role in determining how we perceive our physical appearance and choose our clothes.

Very few people are aware that clothing can be used as a resource to feel more confident, capable and credible.

Do you know that each piece of your garment sends a message?

You might have come across texts online or offline which tells you to 'watch out the message your cloth sends or be careful about the statement you make with your clothes'.

You may have thought it as a marketing gimmick, but actually it is NOT because you do know what the text is talking about.

Clothing is a combination or composition of five elements:

- Lines
- Shapes
- Colour
- Textures
- Fabrics

Each element of the clothing has its own say. In fact, it speaks before you do the talking! Change one detail of an element and you change the message! Amazing, isn't it?

You can always use clothing as a resource benefit.

You can use clothing to influence opinion or action of another person.

Clothing can lift your mood or confidence level.

It can help you create a positive first impression.

Clothing directly affects the way you think, feel and act, and the way others respond to you.

Clothes communicate your personality, attitude, values, interest and mood, just like your body language.

There are four elements in Image Management that are important in selecting clothes:

- **Appropriate:** Select the right clothes according to the occasion. Whether you are a CEO or a homemaker, whether you are at home or on a trip, you are being watched all the time. Therefore, you need to dress accordingly, so that you wear comfort and confidence simultaneously.

- **Authentic:** Be true to yourself and do not turn into someone else when you are around people.

  People are becoming fashion victims in today's world. For this, you can blame social media to some extent. When you blindly copy someone else, it is visible; you may not be comfortable in carrying those clothes or makeup or shoes or the entire look. Then, why just copy when you can build your own comfortable and confident style statement? Every person has his/her own sense of styling. You can go with the trend without leaving your uniqueness. Once you follow the trend, you would never feel outdated; you will only evolve with time.

- **Attractive:** People often compare clothing with self-esteem. The best way to raise your self-esteem instantly is by looking attractive. So, to erase self-doubt, you must make an attempt to look attractive and put your best foot forward because people treat you the way they see you.

- **Affordable:** When I say to look good wear clothes that add the oomph to your personality, that doesn't mean you need to buy branded or designer outfits or dresses. All that you need to do is look good! But how? Simple, you need to choose the tasteful way rather than taking the expensive route. Mind, it's not what we wear, it's how we wear.

Chapter 2

MIX-AND-MATCH TO GET MORE OUT OF YOUR SAME OUTFITS

Deciding what to wear each day is a real challenge for many people, especially for women. Many among you might think that you need a lot of clothes to dress well daily. The truth is- You Don't! You just need a well-planned cluster.

A Cluster is a small group of clothes that work together harmoniously. Let's know more about Cluster:

- Cluster is the mix-and-match of clothes and allows you to build a complete workable wardrobe which will last for years. A well-planned cluster includes enough garments for a variety of looks to fit all your needs.

- Clustering helps you save time, money and energy because you know what you are looking for when you are shopping—pieces that will fit into your existing wardrobe.

- It reduces impulse shopping. Clustering helps you mix your old clothes with newer ones, and you get more outfits from fewer clothes.

- Clustering allows you buy and replace your clothes, a piece or few at a time as fast or slow as your budget and time allow.

- It helps you organise your clothes in new and exciting ways.

- A well-planned cluster helps you spend less time deciding what to wear for different occasions.

Many people have an idea of what mix-and-match looks like and how it works once it's put together but the most common problem people face is how to begin to build a cluster so that they get the results they want. I have simplified it for you.

Cluster guidelines

- Use your favourite colour to create your cluster colour scheme, look for a pattern, print or stripe in your favourite colour. Your print can be on a blouse, shirt, pants, skirt or even an accessory item such as a scarf and tie.

- Choose 5 to 8 pieces, both tops and bottoms to fit your lifestyle. Five pieces might include three tops and two bottoms. The clothes can be new or already existing in your wardrobe. These pieces can be combined to create as many as 12 different looking outfits.

- Begin with pieces that are basic—simple in styles, line and shape. When clothes are simple in style, line and shape, it is easier to combine them for a variety of looks, and they all work well together.

- Select pieces that are distinctly different from one another; no two pieces should be styled alike. Select accessories that go well with the pieces. Gradually, expand your cluster to meet your entire wardrobe.

Chapter 3

COLOUR THAT BEST SUITS YOUR SKIN TONE

The most common question people ask me about colour is: what will best suit my skin tone? Can I wear this colour with that one? When I talk to people about colour, I come to know that people have lots of misconceptions.

Basically, you can wear any colour as per your likes and needs. The colour combinations that you wear, make all the differences.

Remember, every colour, including personal, is relative and may change with lighting, background, clothing and cosmetics.

Personal colour (skin tone, hair and lip colours) changes during your lifetime due to age, diet, health and exposure to the environment. Your colour preferences also change as you mature. You acquire new experience with changes in your goals and lifestyle. Usually, your favourite colours are the ones which form memories of positive experiences of your life.

To appear both harmonious and attractive, you and your clothes should look like they belong together

People often feel tired and bored of clothes they have in their wardrobe due to the monotonous style—either bright colours or dull, muted colours.

Wardrobe neutral colours work best; black, white and grey in their true form are neutral colours.

- Dull, muted tones such as navy blue, burgundy, brown, tan, ivory, olive, teal and plum are wardrobe neutrals. Wardrobe neutrals coordinate well with a large variety of other colours. They do not attract a lot of attention and are understated elegance. Neutral colours are well received, always. People do not get tired of neutral colours quickly.

- Accent colours are bright and strong and may even overpower other colours around them. They create strong dark and light contrast and need special clothes and accessories to complement the outfit.

- Choose a colour that is appropriate for the mood, occasion or activity.

- For formal or business occasions, dull muted colours are usually preferred.

- Bright or accent colours lift the mood for the party and fun activities.

- A good combination of colours in an outfit is usually one neutral and one main colour with an optional small amount of accent colour.

- When combining colours, one must be dominant and all other accessories.

- Dominant colours draw attention, so use them only in places where you want to draw attention and importance.

Chapter 4

DEVELOP YOUR OWN PERSONAL STYLE

Clothing is wearable art. It can stimulate or lift your spirit as much as a painting, song or a sculpture does. Some people have a natural talent or ability to do mix-and-match of different elements of design in appropriate and attractive ways. You can also develop the skill once you learn and practise, and I am sure, you will become more confident and creative about what you choose to wear.

Like any other art, clothing is also a medium of self-expression, individuality and creativity. We all have our sense of style which reflects our personality traits, values, attitude and interests.

Some clothes work better for you because you like the way elements of design are arranged and organised in the outfit; it enhances your appearance. You like the way you look and feel comfortable. The clothes you like and prefer develop into your personal style which largely depends on your lifestyle; it also changes with the change in your way of living, goals and roles.

Mostly, people are not aware of their personal style and hence blindly follow the latest fashion trends.

Personal style is an expression of self rather than the Indiscriminate simulation of the latest fashion trends

Strategies to develop your personal style:

- Create your own style file of favourite looks you find in magazines catalogues and the internet.

- Become aware of what you are wearing, how you feel, act and how others react to your appearance.

- Start experimenting with your clothes to get an idea of what you like, and feel (your comfort level) to develop your personal style.

- Start making little changes at a time. Don't go overboard. You can begin with three different looks with some of your favourite clothes.

If you think you cannot wear bright colours, you can start incorporating a small portion of bright colour in your outfit. For example, if you only wear solid colours, try print or plaid, maybe in your shirt or blouse.

Chapter 5

SHOP SMART AND CHOOSE YOUR PURCHASES WISELY

Open your closet and have a thorough look. Now you have an accurate mental image of all the dresses in your closet. This mental image will give you a direction for planning, shopping, and purchasing wisely. Make a list of items you need to complete your cluster or add further.

Smart shopping skills simplify the shopping process. It saves your time, money and energy. It helps you avoid an accumulation of unnecessary clothes.

Shopping can lift your mood if you feel depressed say some experts

Smart shopping skills:

- Make a list of items you need to complete or add to your cluster.

  Be specific about the item in style, colour and fabric.

- Avoid going for shopping with a group of friends and relatives; you can take one person for a second opinion.

- Don't shop after a day's work or when you are tired and stressed or depressed. It is simply because, on a stressful/hectic day, nothing will look right to you or you might settle for just anything.

- Try not to shop just after eating when your figure is filled out more than usual.

- Dress comfortably and attractively, wear comfortable shoes.

- Wear clothes that slip easily on and off.

Chapter 6

INTRODUCING 7 STEPS OF SELF-TRANSFORMATION TECHNIQUES

With many years of experience and in-depth understanding of the importance of creating the first impression, I have formulated a seven-step self-transformation technique, especially for entrepreneurs, small business owners and individuals.

Seven-step self-transformation techniques work on seven key aspects of clothing, grooming, body language, etiquette, communication, time management and interpersonal skills to improve your overall image skill sets and presentation style.

I assure you, once you go through it, you will see an unstoppable New You. It will enable you eliminate self-doubt, become confident, fulfill your goals and achieve success in your personal, professional and social life.